Original title:
Wristbands of Wisdom

Copyright © 2025 Creative Arts Management OÜ
All rights reserved.

Author: Helena Marchant
ISBN HARDBACK: 978-1-80586-132-4
ISBN PAPERBACK: 978-1-80586-604-6

Adornments of the Mind

On my wrist, I wear a thought,
A little band that's tightly caught.
It whispers jokes I can't resist,
In meetings, it's the perfect twist.

Each color tells a silly tale,
Of mishaps, laughter, and a snail.
They say wisdom comes with age,
I say it comes in fabric stage.

Symbols of Sage

I've got a bright red band for glee,
It makes me laugh, just look and see!
A blue one gives advice quite wise,
To never take a snack from flies.

Orange is for when I'm a clown,
It lifts my mood when I wear it down.
Green's the shade for nature's call,
Just don't wear it while at the mall!

Chronicles in Fabric

My wrist is a museum, don't you know?
With tales of folly and a friendly show.
One's from a party, someone spilled a drink,
Now it reminds me not to think!

Another's from when I tried to dance,
Tripped on air—oh, what a chance!
These threads of memory I won't lose,
In every color, I get to choose.

Wearables of Wisdom

Each band a puzzle, piecing laughs,
In public gatherings, it always wafts.
My friends all giggle, point, and tease,
Not knowing I'm the one who sees!

With bows and bliss, I strut around,
Each twist of wrist holds joy profound.
Wearables give me wisdom's tune,
As I walk through life, more like a loon.

Emblems of Insight

A rubber band stretched tight and neat,
Tells you to dance, not just retreat.
It whispers jokes, elevates the day,
And makes wisecracks in a quirky way.

With every twist, it bounces cheer,
"Don't take yourself too seriously, my dear!"
Funny reminders, snug on your wrist,
A playful nudge that can't be missed.

Adornments of Awareness

A colorful band, a sight to behold,
It stays on tight, never gets old.
It winks at your thoughts, "Stay alert, stay jolly!"
"Even wise folks can act quite folly!"

A joke in its stretch, a laugh in its bend,
An accessory that keeps wisdom as a friend.
When life gets tough, and smiles are few,
Just take a glance and chuckle anew.

Clasps of Comprehension

This little loop holds secrets galore,
It giggles in truth, while asking for more.
A clasp of insight, oh what a delight,
Wraps around wrists, makes humor ignite.

"Did you hear the one about the fish?"
It teases your mind, makes you laugh, that's the wish.
It knows the punchlines, it knows the puns,
A fun little band that brightens the runs.

Symbols of Sages

A charm with a grin, it spins with flair,
Holds quirky knowledge, ready to share.
"Why did the chicken cross the road?" it beams,
"Don't ponder so much, just follow your dreams!"

It rests on your wrist, adorned with style,
Bringing laughter and wisdom, all in a while.
A playful reminder, a vibrant assist,
Life is more fun with a twist of a wrist!

Emblems of Enlightenment

A band of colors wraps my wrist,
Each shade a thought, none can resist.
Red means pizza, that's a treat,
While blue just signals, take a seat.

Green for wisdom, or maybe grass,
Yellow screams, 'Boy, you've got some sass!'
They jingle when I raise my hand,
Funny little symbols, all are grand.

Gifts of Grace

These little gifts, they dance and twirl,
Each color shines, ready to unfurl.
Orange for laughter, what a surprise,
Pink means hugs, as fun as fries!

Gold for riches, though I'm quite broke,
Purple for mischief, here's a joke!
They're like my thoughts, all tied in knots,
Gifts of grace without the slots.

Interwoven Ideals

Tangled thoughts on my wrist do play,
Like a circus clown in bright display.
A twist of fate, a slip of chance,
Pink and green join in a dance.

Here's a red one for the sushi night,
And blue for sleep, oh what a sight!
Jubilant threads with wisdom twined,
Interwoven dreams in colors defined.

The Fabric of Thought

Threads of laughter sewn with care,
Stitched together, life's a dare.
Orange joke wraps the wrist so tight,
While gray brings wisdom, out of sight.

A fabric that bends to every whim,
Each thought a color, each laugh a hymn.
With twinkling charms that jingle and sway,
This tapestry of thoughts brightens my day.

Tapestry of Truth

In a world so vast and wide,
We wear our tales like a wild ride.
Threads of laughter woven tight,
Stitching wisdom day and night.

With each color, a story to share,
Follies and blunders, beyond compare.
Tangles of wisdom, humor bright,
Woven together, a glorious sight.

Ribbons of Resolve

A ribbon tied, a promise made,
With jokes and jests, we're never played.
We dance through life, a lively twirl,
Each knot a giggle, each laugh a pearl.

In every twist, a lesson learned,\nAs we prance around, our courage burned.
With colorful ribbons, we stand bold,
In the hilarity of life, we're gold!

Knots of Knowledge

Tangled knots by the old oak tree,
Each one whispers a secret, oh so free.
In tangles tight, hilarity reigns,
Wisdom found in our silly chains.

With playful jests and winks, we tie,
Life's funny lessons make us fly high.
Every knot spins a tale so grand,
Laughter and knowledge go hand in hand.

Stories Worn

We wear our humor like a badge,
Each story a laugh, never a fad.
In the fabric of life, we stitch and sew,
Tales of mischief that always glow.

With every thread, a chuckle found,
In the chaos of life, we stand our ground.
Stories worn like a favorite tee,
Together we laugh, just you and me.

Labyrinths of Learning

In a maze of thoughts, I roam,
Finding breadcrumbs on my own.
Each twist and turn, a lesson learned,
A quirky path where wisdom's burned.

Socks go missing, wisdom's gain,
In the tumble dryer, it's insane!
Flip the script, it's all a game,
Laughter bubbles, and I'm to blame.

The book of life, a bit askew,
With doodles of the things I brew.
Pages flutter, knowledge flies,
I wear my quirks like funny ties.

Patterns of the Past

Stumbling on old shoelace tales,
Retro fashion, friend or fails?
Polka dots and plaid collide,
Hilarious history, no need to hide.

Memories tangled like spaghetti mess,
Try to untwist, but what a dress!
Each outfit worn, a story shared,
With laughter echoes, no one spared.

The mirror shows the fashion woes,
But in the heart, color grows.
Patterned paths where smiles abide,
Dancing footsteps, wisdom wide.

Threads of Insight

A needle's eye and endless thread,
Stitching thoughts that dance in bed.
With every knot, a new reside,
Clever quirks, my humor's guide.

Looping laughter in every seam,
Dreams unravel, or so it seems.
My fabric's patchwork, wild and bright,
Woven tales that spark delight.

In fields of yarn, I take a dash,
Stitch a joke, then make a splash.
With every tug, a giggle tight,
Threads of insight, woven light.

Bracelets of Experience

A jingle jangle on my wrist,
Each charm a tale, you can't resist.
From shiny beads to secrets wrapped,
Life's funny moments all mapped.

Each clink and clank, a memory spins,
Doodads that tell of my goofy wins.
Amusing tales in bracelets stacked,
With every twist, a laugh's unpacked.

Strapped with joy, my life's parade,
From fumbles made to pranks displayed.
With blingy wit, I walk my way,
Experience shines bright every day.

Threads of Tradition

In a world of colors bright,
A wrist of fabric feels so right.
Each thread a tale, we wear with pride,
Old quirks and laughs forever tied.

Dance and twirl, let laughter flow,
Each wrap a secret only we know.
From grandmas' tales to silly gaffes,
A bunch of charms that make us laugh.

Straps of Serenity

Worn like a secret hug so tight,
Hiding joys in morning light.
Each loop a calm, a soothing day,
To chase the mundane far away.

Jokes sewn within each little knot,
Reminders of the silly spots.
With every twist, we find our peace,
A giggle here, and woes release.

Dangles of Discovery

Swinging charms that jingle loud,
With each shake, we join the crowd.
A hunt for laughs in every chime,
In every knotted twist, pure rhyme.

From silly sayings that we quote,
To doodles that we proudly tote.
Adventure beckons with each fling,
Who knew wisdom could be such a thing?

Messages in Motion

Life's a game—let's play pretend,
With every twist, a message to send.
Giggle and wiggle, sway to the beat,
These colorful wraps can't be beat!

With every spin, a new surprise,
Who knew wisdom could be so wise?
In the shuffle of life, a silly toast,
To the bonds we cherish the very most.

Strands of Knowledge

A tale of pearls, and strings of thread,
We wear these charms atop our head.
From grandma's quips to dad's old jokes,
Each strand a giggle, sparks and pokes.

In twinkling hues, they dance with glee,
A rainbow's wisdom, wild and free.
When life gets messy, like spilled juice,
These threads of thought give us a moose!

Bracelets of Belief

Around our wrists, the charms parade,
In every twist, a joke is laid.
Wear one for daytime, one for night,
A motto here, a pun in sight.

If you lose one, don't feel despair,
Just tie on laughter, shake your hair.
Each dangle tells of moments grand,
With wit and whimsy, life's well planned.

Adages Embraced

New sayings bloom like flowers in spring,
Each phrase a dance, a quirky fling.
"Why did the chicken?" starts the lore,
With laughs galore, who could want more?

We clutch these gems, with joy they shed,
Spreading wisdom, as jokes are fed.
From knock-knock zingers to quips with flair,
Happiness grows, floating in air.

Insights in Color

A dash of purple, a pinch of green,
In every hue, wisdom's seen.
Like candy-coated thoughts on a string,
We munch on laughs that memories bring.

Orange skies with yellow beams,
A burst of joy inside our dreams.
Funny bones tickle, oh what a sight,
With insights bright, we laugh all night!

Chains of Understanding

In life, we wear our links so bright,
Heavy truths feel ever light.
With jingles and jangles, we strut about,
Understanding floats, let's all shout out!

Wearing wisdom on a whim,
Our lives are not so grim.
With each new chain, we crack a grin,
Come join the fun, let's all dive in!

Life's puzzles, we solve with flair,
In colorful chains, without a care.
Dancing thoughts, they twist and sway,
Understanding's game we love to play!

So grab your chains, don't be shy,
Let's connect our thoughts up high!
With giggles and laughs, we're never lost,
In the web of wisdom, we're the topmost!

Cuffs of Clarity

Slap on these cuffs, embrace the jest,
In confusion's game, we're truly blessed.
Questions bounce like rubber balls,
Clarity shines through all our walls!

With each light tug, we pull more clear,
Knots of thoughts untangle near.
Like juggling clowns, we twist and spin,
Cuffs of clarity, let the fun begin!

What's that? A thought, a giggle here?
In silly cuffs, we all cheer!
We stack our dreams, so high, so tall,
Clarity laughs, we just can't stall!

So wear your cuffs, join the parade,
Reckless fun in wisdom's shade.
With clarity's light, our worries fade,
In a world of giggles, we're all remade!

Bands of Reflection

Let's strap on bands, so shiny and fun,
Reflecting smiles, our work is done.
In muddled thoughts, we find a way,
Bands of reflection, come join the play!

With every twist, our minds expand,
We dance through life, it's always grand.
Mirror, mirror, who's the best?
In humor's realm, we ace the test!

Our thoughts bounce back, a funny sight,
In bands of reflection, we take flight.
Laughter peeks through every crack,
Let's wear these bands, there's no lack!

So gather round, let's have a laugh,
In these bands, we find our path.
With reflective joy, we dance and sway,
In the spirit of fun, we'll seize the day!

Links of Knowledge

Chain me up with knowledge bold,
In links of laughter, break the mold.
Each nugget shines, a gem of gold,
In this wild dance, we find our hold!

Link by link, we craft the tale,
Tickle our minds, we shall not fail.
With each wisecrack, wisdom flows,
In fun-filled moments, it surely grows!

And in this chain, we twist and shout,
Links of knowledge, with zero doubt.
Each joke we share is a learning spree,
A lesson wrapped in hilarity!

So grab those links and let them shine,
In this clever chain, let's intertwine.
With knowledge sparkling, laughter's glee,
In this joyful life, we're totally free!

Inscribed Lessons

On the wrist, tales from the past,
Where laughter and mishaps are cast.
Each twist and turn, a silly thought,
Lessons learned, but often forgot.

With a flick of the wrist, we recall,
The time someone tripped and did fall.
Like a charm, memories play,
Reminding us joy's just a slip away.

Patterns of Perception

Like stripes on a shirt, some days we see,
Life's a puzzle, a quirky spree.
From polka dots to wavy lines,
Each moment we live, in laughter it shines.

The twists and turns, all part of the game,
In this circus of life, we're all a bit lame.
Embrace the fun, let patterns collide,
In the fabric of humor, we all take pride.

Charms of Clarity

A tiny trinket to brighten the day,
Reminding us to laugh and to play.
When wisdom's wrapped in a silly disguise,
We find the truth in the laughter that lies.

Beneath the glitter, there's wisdom to share,
In moments of chaos, it's light as air.
So wear your charms, let them jiggle and swing,
In the dance of life, humor's the king!

Tapestry of Time

Thread by thread, we weave our lore,
In the fabric of life, we always want more.
With a snicker and giggle, we stitch our fate,
Moments of joy, never too late.

From each little knot, a story unfolds,
In the colors of laughter, life never grows old.
So spin the yarn, let your heart shine bright,
In this tapestry of time, make humor your light.

Fragments of Faith

In a world so wobbly, we stumble and trip,
With giggles and grins, we learn how to flip.
A splash of mischief, perhaps a small fight,
Faith's just a punchline, with laughter so bright.

We juggle our dreams with a whimsical flair,
Wobbling wildly as we dance through the air.
Every little fumble, a lesson in disguise,
Faith's just a nudge with a wink in our eyes.

So raise up your glass of fizzy delight,
Let's toast to the misfits who shine in the night.
With faith wrapped in laughter, we boldly proclaim,
That life's but a jest; we're all in the game.

Essence of Experience

In a carnival of blunders, we ride the wild ride,
With cotton candy thoughts, and marshmallow pride.
The lessons we learn from the slips and the falls,
Are treasures that glimmer like vibrant street stalls.

With every grand tale of loot that we hold,
Are quirks and mishaps that turned into gold.
Our misadventures are the real VIPs,
Sprinkled with laughter like a summer breeze.

We dance with our dreams, twirling like sprites,
Savoring moments, oh what pure delights.
Experience is a giggle with a twist of a grin,
Join this merry fair; let the fun begin.

Shards of Serenity

In a world of chaos, serenity glows,
With giggles and chuckles, tranquility flows.
A calmness to capture, with humor so light,
Like whispers of mischief in the soft twilight.

We ride quirky waves, on marshmallow clouds,
While spinning on teacups in jovial crowds.
Serenity's secret? A chuckle or two,
And never forget to snicker at you!

We sprinkle our paths with whimsy's best charms,
Finding peace in the chaos, embracing the harms.
So smile as we wander, life's a merry spree,
With shards of sweet laughter, we're wild and free!

Armbands of Aspirations

With dreams like balloons, we aim for the sky,
Tethered to giggles, we launch and we fly.
Aspirations in pockets, like candy we share,
Dipped in humor's nectar, they dance in the air.

We wear our ambitions like hats turned askew,
They squeak with delight, in this hullabaloo.
Each quirk a reminder to dream and aspire,
With laughter our fuel, we never tire.

So gather your wishes, let's throw them around,
With a flick and a giggle, they'll soar off the ground.
Aspirations are jokes that we're together to make,
In this circus of life, let's dance and awake!

Chronicles in Color

In a world of bracelets bright,
Each hue holds a quirky bite.
Red for laughter, blue for glee,
Green for snacks, come share with me.

Orange whispers tales of fun,
Yellow's shines like the sun.
Pink is for the silly dance,
Turn it up, let's take a chance!

Purple says, "Don't take it tough!"
While gray just chuckles, "Enough is enough."
Together they jive, twist and twirl,
These bands of joy, oh what a whirl!

So slap on colors, loud and proud,
Join the laughter, sing it loud.
Lessons wrapped in vibrant cheer,
Chronicles spun, year after year.

Lattice of Life Lessons

Strands of humor, woven tight,
Life's a comedy, what a sight!
Each knot a giggle, each twist a grin,
Embrace the silliness, let's begin!

In one corner, there's a jest,
Another holds a little quest.
Tie them all in a delightful mess,
A lattice crafted from pure finesse.

Colors clash, yet they belong,
Sing along to a catchy song.
A tapestry of tales in thread,
Where every laugh embraces dread.

So grab your friends and let's create,
A funky weave, it's never late.
These lessons taught with a wink and grin,
In this lattice, we all win!

Weaves of Wisdom

On the fabric of our days,
Laughter weaves through, in funny ways.
A twist of fate, a colorful thread,
Silliness where our worries fled.

Each loop's a story, sly and sly,
The zany moments can't pass by.
In vibrant tones they play their part,
A patchwork quilt to warm the heart.

With every hue an insight bright,
Life's dance is silly, pure delight.
So let your spirit jive and sway,
As we weave our wisdom into play.

Hold fast to humor, light and free,
In these threads of giggles, joy you'll see.
Embrace the silly, let it flow,
For in this fabric, we all glow!

Charms of Change

Each charm a story, wild and bold,
Secrets of laughter, yet untold.
A jingle here, a jangle there,
Bracelet dreams float in the air.

Lost your keys? Just laugh it off,
Remember the giggles when you scoff.
Life's a jigsaw, bits and parts,
Cherished moments fill our hearts.

Swinging charms that twist and spin,
Each a reminder of where we've been.
Tales of fumbles and silly fails,
Trinkets of change, where laughter prevails.

So wear your charms and shake it out,
Life's a journey, without a doubt.
In every turn, chuckles greet,
As we find wisdom in life's beat!

Crowns of Conscience

A crown of thought sits atop my head,
Made of rubber bands, it's a bright thread.
It bounces with laughter, never grown dull,
A sassy reminder, my mind's at a lull.

Each colored band holds a silly tale,
Of pizza dreams and a whale named Gale.
I wear them with pride, like silly fools,
Each twist of fate breaks all the rules.

If wisdom's a game, I sport the best gear,
Joking with friends, spreading pure cheer.
They laugh and they grin, as I take a bow,
With my crown of wit, I rule this town.

In nights of joy, our minds all align,
With crowns of laughter, we're doing just fine.
A kingdom of chuckles, oh what a dream,
With this revolting wisdom—it's all a meme!

Choices in Closure

A choice to make, oh what a delight,
Flip a coin or go with the sight?
I wear my choices like shoes too tight,
Each step clumsy, but keeps the night bright.

In the land of options, I dance and I sway,
Every wrong turn, a new game to play.
"Should I wear polka dots or stripes today?"
The world giggles on this topsy-turvy way.

Now pick a path, which will it be?
Maybe both, in a kooky spree!
Choices all jumbled, like socks in a wash,
I wear mismatched dreams with a smile and a swash.

So if you're unsure, just take a chance,
Wear your choices like a pantsless dance.
In laughter and fun, we'll surely find,
That silly decisions can free the mind!

Adornments of Authenticity

My bling shimmers bright, oh what a sight,
Wearing quirks like badges, they feel just right.
With glitter and glam, I strutted so proud,
Authentic adornments, funny and loud.

Each doodle and doodad tells tales of my heart,
A cape made of mess, my own work of art.
In a world of mirrors, I choose to be me,
With charms made of laughter and whimsy's decree.

I twirl through the streets, giggles in tow,
My fancy attire makes joy overflow.
Who needs all the bling, the diamonds, the gold?
When colorful laughter is the treasure to hold!

So embrace all your quirks, let your true self shine,
Adornments of glee, what a great design!
In this funny parade, we all find our place,
With silly authenticity, we embrace the space.

Chronicles of Curiosity

A curious cat, with eyes big and wide,
Exploring my thoughts, I take a wild ride.
I pry at the hinges of this crazy world,
With each silly query, my dreams are unfurled.

What if socks could talk? Oh, the tales they'd tell,
Of journeys through laundry, and trips to the well.
With giggles and gaffes, I wander away,
In my realm of wonder, it's a quirky display.

Questions like kites, they soar through the air,
"Why don't ducks wear pants?" Life's riddles to share!
With laughter abound, curiosity grows,
In a garden of whims, anything goes!

So join in the fun, let your brain spin around,
In chronicles silly, new marvels are found.
As curiosity blossoms like flowers in spring,
We're all just explorers—oh, what joy it can bring!

Balances of Being

In life's game of twister, we all spin,
With left hand on blue, and a grin within.
We jump and we twist, in the weirdest dance,
Flexibility's key, if we get the chance.

Juggling our hopes like a circus act,
Dropping the balls isn't a complete fact.
With laughter and pasta, we'll mix our fate,
Add a pinch of joy, it's never too late.

A balance of chaos and awkward grace,
Like trying to catch a balloon in space.
We stumble and giggle, take it in stride,
Let's spin through our blunders with hearts open wide.

Meditation in Motion

In the stillness of chaos, we find our flow,
Wiggling our toes where the wild breezes blow.
With eyes closed tightly, we lose all our care,
While doing a dance that's both silly and rare.

We float down the street on a cloud of delight,
Trying to balance on the edge of night.
With thoughts like confetti, they swirl and they twist,
Each giggle of wisdom, just cannot be missed.

A somersault through life's zany routine,
Finding some laughter in every scene.
With a leap and a bounce, we're tumbling free,
Spreading our joy like a leaf from a tree.

Halo of Harmony

With halos all askew, we dance in a line,
Chasing our shadows as if they were wine.
We twirl and we whirl, like a funky brigade,
Collecting our smiles in a joyful parade.

The soundtrack of chuckles fills up the air,
We laugh 'til we wheeze, with no room for care.
In this circle of giggles, we find our light,
Wobbling together, oh, what a sight!

Harmony's here, in slapstick delight,
For every misstep is a reason to write.
We'll sing off-key and skip like a stone,
Together we're goofy, never alone.

Keepsakes of Kindness

With pockets of kindness, we gather our loot,
Trading warm smiles like a sweet, fruity fruit.
A giggle exchanged for a high-five or two,
Creates a ripple, just like morning dew.

In a world where we trip on our shoelace of fun,
Each tumble we take shows the kindness we've spun.
We collect all our laughter like marbles in hand,
Rolling through life, oh, isn't it grand?

Each keepsake we cherish becomes our delight,
Filling our hearts with warmth, shining bright.
Let's wear our mishaps like badges in style,
Crafting a life that's quirky all the while.

Pulse of Philosophy

In a world where thoughts collide,
Witty minds take the wild ride.
With laughter echoing through the air,
Questions float without a care.

Philosophers in silly hats,
Debating cats and playful rats.
They ponder life over cups of tea,
While munching on a slice of brie.

A jester joins—a twisty sage,
Dances on the wisdom stage.
Each giggle sparks a thought anew,
Philosophy, with a fun hue.

With every chuckle, truths unfold,
In laughter, our minds grow bold.
So let the questions take their flight,
In wit, we find the sheer delight.

Wisps of Wisdom

A feather floats upon the breeze,
Whispers of truth among the trees.
In playful tones, the sparrows sing,
As wisdom dangles from a string.

Old sages in a game of charades,
Playing tricks in the sunlit glades.
They toss around their clever quips,
With twinkling eyes and silly skips.

A fortune cookie made of cheese,
Spouts proverbs sure to please.
Each brittle laugh brings insight near,
As nonsense drips with wisdom clear.

So grab a giggle, take a stand,
Let joy and knowledge hand in hand.
For every wise crack and jest,
Is life's little riddle, at its best.

Strands of Serenity

In a world where Zen wears a hat,
Knitting peace with a joyful chat.
Serenity dances on a breeze,
Tickling the minds of buzzing bees.

Meditation? Just a trendy show,
With mats arranged in rows of woe.
But laughter fills each quiet space,
As wisecracks slip with gentle grace.

Yoga poses gone awry,
Downward dog meets the lopsided sky.
In every bend and hapless fall,
Tranquility finds a giggling call.

So here's to calm in every jest,
Where mirth and peace can both invest.
We twist and turn through laughter's maze,
Finding joy in tranquil ways.

Links of Legacy

A chain of laughter woven tight,
Links of wisdom shine so bright.
Each joke passed down, a treasured tome,
In every chuckle, we find our home.

Grandpa's tales with a punchline twist,
History masked in a fun-fueled mist.
With every story, the past takes flight,
Creating bonds that feel just right.

From silly pranks to wise old advice,
Life's quirky legacy is quite nice.
Like a string of pearls, we wear our glee,
Each laugh connecting you and me.

So let's embrace this playful thread,
Where humor dances, joy is fed.
In laughter's arms, together we blend,
Building links that never end.

Strands of Enlightenment

In a world of chatter, we wear our guide,
Colorful threads hold secrets inside.
One spark of wisdom, a silly cheer,
Unraveling truths, oh look, a deer!

Laughing at life with each little twist,
We dance around topics, not one can resist.
With every knot tied, another joke shared,
Lessons learned lightly, we're all unprepared.

From multicolors bright, we craft a new tale,
Every misstep leads to a funny fail.
Sipping on wisdom, like juice from a cup,
When things get too serious, we just light up!

So roll with the quirks, let laughter set free,
A tapestry woven with glee and esprit.
For laughter's the secret, easy to find,
In colorful strands that loop in your mind.

Ties of Truth

With ties wrapped tightly, we promise to share,
Each funky adventure, a truth laid bare.
Tug on a string, let the giggles begin,
For wisdom is funny, let's all dive in!

We walk in circles, with socks mismatched,
Truths stained with laughter, our funbook attached.
Every twist and turn, brings chuckles anew,
With each stretch of fabric, we tease out the true.

From friendly advice, to a quirk in a joke,
Underneath our ties, there's wisdom bespoke.
With every tug, a giggle, we glean,
Who needs a sage when you have this scene?

So gather 'round, friends, let's tie up some fun,
Truths laced with laughter, let the good times run.
On this wobbly road, may we always be brave,
With ties of our making, let's dance on the wave.

Ribbons of Insight

In ribbons so bright, we dance with delight,
Each twist tells a story, a shared little plight.
Unraveling laughter, we weave it with style,
Wisdom is better when wrapped with a smile.

"Watch where you're going!" a friend shouts with glee,
"You'll trip on a ribbon, just wait, you'll see!"
Every tumble and fall is a lesson in jest,
Ribbons of insight make life feel the best.

From the lines that we tie, let's spin tales untold,
A patchwork of moments that sparkle like gold.
With each little knot, let's giggle and sing,
For laughter and wisdom are the same jolly thing.

So gather your ribbons, and dance in the breeze,
Fun's in the mix, like a warm bowl of cheese.
With colorful threads that don't always conform,
We learn with a chuckle, each note in our swarm.

Tokens of Thought

With tokens in hand, we barter for smiles,
Trading good humor for compassion in piles.
A slapstick moment, a comedic exchange,
Tokens of thought make the weird feel so strange.

Each token a memory, silly and sweet,
A wink and a nudge, just can't be beat.
Through laughter, we ponder, and ponder some more,
Finding wisdom in punchlines behind every door.

As we toss our tokens, some silly, some wise,
We chase down the laughter, let humor arise.
Through quips and through quirks, we fashion our fate,
Each chuckle a lesson, isn't life great?

So come on, my friends, let's trade and concat,
Tokens of thought, like a well-worn hat.
For the world's more fun when we share a good joke,
With a wink and a nudge, let's spark our own smoke!

Medallions of Memory

Round and shiny, oh what a treat,
They jingle and jangle with every heartbeat.
No treasure map, just a whimsical quest,
Chasing the past, we're humorously blessed.

Grandma's stories, they come with a flair,
Like socks and sandals, our fashion's a scare.
Each jingle a giggle, a chuckle or two,
Reminding us fondly, we've all been a zoo.

Funky colors, unique in design,
These trinkets of laughter are simply divine.
With every mishap, and every regret,
We wear them with pride, like a birthday pet.

So here's to the memories, those quirks in our past,
They whizz by like time, yet they always last.
In our silly collection, with glee we abide,
These knickknacks of moments are our fun, bona fide!

Threads of Tradition

Stitched in laughter, woven with care,
Glittery tales that we love to share.
Mixing patterns, some wild, some nice,
In the fabric of life, we toss in some spice.

Granny's secrets and Uncle Lou's dance,
Tangled up tightly, an accidental chance.
As we twirl through the years, it's a slapstick show,
With every tug on the thread, off we go!

Tassels and trinkets all hang with pride,
Holding onto moments, beaming wide-eyed.
In layers of laughter, we find our way back,
To jingling joys that we never lack.

So here's to our stitching, so quirky and bold,
A tapestry of giggles, a sight to behold.
Through every misstep and unkempt twist,
We wear our traditions with a giggly twist!

Wisdom's Embrace

Huddled together, like grandpa's old chair,
Finding wisdom in each silly affair.
With each goofy toss, and clumsy fall,
Laughter's the trophy, we cherish it all.

Ticklish moments, springing up fast,
Forget all the rules; we're having a blast!
In the coziness of folly, we snuggle and grin,
As the wisdom of laughter pulls us all in.

Jokes told in whispers, secrets to keep,
Those gleeful giggles, oh, they run deep.
Through frolic and folly, let's keep it embraced,
In this dance of hilarity, life's never unchaste.

So let's hold onto joy, with arms open wide,
With laughter as guide, it's a whimsical ride.
For in each silly story, the best part's the tease,
The wisdom of chuckles is sure to please!

Iconic Intuition

In a world of chaos, we stumble and sway,
Dancing through mishaps in a comical way.
Fumbling about with a grin ear to ear,
Our iconic instincts make laughter appear.

From fashion faux pas to karaoke night,
We strut our stuff, never scared of the light.
Like clowns in a circus, pure joy we convey,
With each playful pratfall, we brightened the day.

A wink here, a nod there, our flair on display,
Creating a ruckus; it's our own cabaret.
In the rhythm of folly, we find our own truth,
With quirky decisions, reminiscent of youth.

So here's to our antics, wild and unplanned,
With the spirit of laughter, we boldly stand.
Through every goof-up, and slight miscalculation,
We turn it to humor: a true celebration!

Cuffs of Courage

In a world so big and bold,
I wear my cuffs, or so I'm told.
They gleam with charm, they sparkle bright,
Bringing laughter, day and night.

When I face fear, I give a shout,
These cuffs will help me sort it out.
I strut and dance, a goofy flair,
With silly moves beyond compare.

They jingle loud like cats in heat,
Every time I jump on my feet.
My friends all giggle, roll their eyes,
But I'm the one who's brave and wise!

So here's to courage, made of fun,
With every laugh, I've already won.
With cuffs so lively, come join the spree,
A party of bravery, just you and me!

Pearls of Patience

I found some pearls in the kitchen sink,
They shimmer and shine, oh, what do you think?
As I wait in line, my eyes start to roll,
But these radiant gems kept me in control.

I juggle my tasks like a circus clown,
While waiting for coffee, as time trickles down.
My pearls remind me, slow down the chase,
And with every sip, I find my own space.

Each pearl a reminder that life takes its time,
To savor the moments that taste like a rhyme.
I crack jokes with patience, as folks tap their feet,
Unraveling laughter, oh what a treat!

So here's to the pearls, shiny and round,
In moments of stillness, a joy can be found.
In laughter, we meet—let's not be too tense,
With pearls of patience, life's a fun suspense!

Gems of Growth

In my garden, they bloom and sprout,
With every giggle, I'm turning about.
These gems of growth shine ever so bright,
They sparkle with wisdom, a hilarious sight.

As I water the plants with a bucket of cheer,
They dance with the wind, let's all disappear!
With each little sprout, I sing out loud,
Embracing the goofiness, feeling so proud.

They whisper to me when I trip and fall,
"Get up, my friend! It's just part of the ball!"
So I laugh through the dirt, and I dance with the weeds,
With gems of growth, I plant joyful seeds.

In the garden of life, we all must evolve,
With giggles and grins, our problems dissolve.
Join in the fun, with laughter to share,
With gems of growth, we float without care!

Signets of Serenity

I wear my signets, not on my hands,
But in my mind, oh, isn't it grand?
Each little chuckle, each silly remark,
Turns chaos to calm, ignites a spark.

When life gets frantic, I gently breathe,
With signets of peace, I charm and weave.
In moments of chaos, I wobble and sway,
Creating my calm in a funny ballet.

They twirl and they spin, as I sip my tea,
My signets remind me, just let it be!
The world may be wild, with twists and with turns,
But with every chuckle, inner peace burns.

So here's to the joy that comes from within,
With signets of serenity, let the fun begin!
In the dance of tranquility, we all can unite,
Embracing the laughter, our hearts feel so light!

Jewels of Jaded Souls

In the corners of my brain, a sparkle glows,
A gem of laughter, where the funny flows.
I wear my quirks like medals of pride,
Dancing through life, my humor's my guide.

From socks that don't match to hair that's askew,
Each gem sparkles bright, a comedy cue.
I collect oddities, a treasure so vast,
Making life's mischief a glorious blast.

Puns are my jewels, they shine and they wink,
Turning everyday woes to giggles, I think.
Each chuckle's a jewel, each grin a delight,
Jaded souls witness a comic's insight.

So wear your oddities, let laughter be told,
For the spark of joy is worth more than gold.
In this life's jigsaw, just let your heart play,
And find your own jewels in the mess of each day.

Chains of the Mind

In the labyrinth of thoughts, a crazy parade,
Chained ideas spark like the sun's warm cascade.
I trip over logic, but laugh as I fall,
Each clumsy misstep, a giggle-filled brawl.

Link by link, my thoughts take a ride,
On rollercoasters where silliness hides.
Banana peels scatter, as wisdom goes wild,
In chains of the mind, we're all just a child.

Overthinking? Nah, it's a carnival ride,
Where clowns throw confetti and logic must hide.
With each twist and turn, absurdity reigns,
Laughing, we dance through our whimsical chains.

So gather your chains, let the fun intertwine,
In this circus of thought, let your laughter shine.
For in every wild turn, a truth we shall find,
That joy's just a whim of the chains of the mind.

Mantras In Motion

Swaying like bamboo, with mantras we sing,
In a dance of humor, let wildness take wing.
Each wacky expression, a mantra, a chant,
In this circus of life, we all do a slant.

With every silly wiggle, our worries take flight,
Letting laughter ripple into the night.
Jokes become mantras that sway to the beat,
While life's jester's rhythm keeps us on our feet.

Flip-flops and giggles lead us down joy's road,
Creating a movement, embracing the load.
Each chuckle a mantra that springs from the heart,
In motion, we find where the fun really starts.

So leap and so twirl, in this mantra-filled dance,
Together we prance as we leap at a chance.
In life's wacky rhythm, remember the thrill,
To flow is to giggle, to laugh is to chill.

Charms of Perspective

With quirky charms, I jingle and sway,
Each trinket a giggle, a bright sunny ray.
I spin tales of folly from dusk until dawn,
Finding joy in the chaos, my laughter's my pawn.

From the view that's all twisted, I see the bright side,
A cupcake of wisdom with sprinkles, I ride.
Collecting perspectives like rare little finds,
Sprouting smiles and giggles in fantastical minds.

Those charms on my bracelet tell stories so bright,
Of mishaps and laughter that dance in the light.
Where reason takes naps, and whimsy takes charge,
In the mix of our chaos, we all seem so large.

So gather your charms, let your heart be the guide,
For the funny is there, if we open wide.
In perspectives of laughter, we find our delight,
In life's quirky journey, let your soul take flight.

Medallions of Memory

Once I wore a pretty charm,
But it vanished; oh, such harm!
My memory, as fickle as a cat,
Said it's hiding under the mat!

Pictures of my silly dance,
Stuck in my head, lost in a trance,
Medallions jingle, tales so grand,
If only my memory was less bland!

Old stories turn into tall tales,
Like fish that grow with every gale,
At gatherings, I've earned my fame,
For making each retelling a game!

Now I jot down every quirk,
In a notebook that's quite a perk,
With doodles of the fun we had,
For chasing lost thoughts, I'm not sad!

Remembrances on the Wrist

A colorful band, a winkle in time,
Each one marks a reason or rhyme,
From pizza nights to gym fails galore,
All tangled up like a friendly chore!

Bracelets telling tales so absurd,
Each wrist a library, haven't you heard?
From laundry mishaps to coffee spills,
Adventures of life that always thrill!

I wear my memories like a badge,
Of laughing until I'm in a rage,
Each loop and twist a laugh, a jest,
Friends say "That one's the very best!"

So I gather all that joy and play,
With each remembrance, I find my way,
Every slip and sunshine beaming,
Life's a dance, and I'm still dreaming!

Adornments of Intellect

In the realm of wit, I'd proudly boast,
Adornments wear wisdom like a ghost,
A maze of facts and funny bluffs,
Who knew knowledge could be such fluff?

Put on a hat—oh, look at me!
A walking brain, or so they see,
But underneath this crown of lore,
I trip on my thoughts, oh, what a chore!

With ribbons of logic tied around tight,
I ponder day and dream at night,
Jokes intertwined with facts so cool,
Yet I answer wrong when played the fool!

Wise guys chuckle and nod in glee,
For even the smartest sometimes see,
It's all a game, a playful jest,
And I'm the jester, wearing my quest!

Expressions of Enlightenment

On my wrist, you'll find the glow,
Of something wise, or just a show,
Expressions gleam, with each bright hue,
In laughter, there's learning—who knew?

So I dance with the quirks of fate,
Stumble into wisdom and debate,
With every giggle, knowledge springs,
Who said enlightenment lacked fun things?

Each band a riddle, a puzzle to trace,
I try to keep up the dizzy pace,
For life's a circus, and I'm the star,
Spinning wisdom with a laughter jar!

So join me here, in this joyful spree,
Where enlightenment's meant to be free,
And with a chuckle, we shall proclaim,
That wisdom's just a funny game!

Echoes of Experience

In a world of lessons grand,
We wear our silly thoughts like bands.
Each memory makes us laugh aloud,
As we share our stories, feeling proud.

From mishaps that made our faces red,
To wisdom that's always misled.
We stumble and trip on our own two feet,
Yet each fall results in laughter sweet.

A blunder here, a goof over there,
Our lessons dance like they just don't care.
With every slip, we find our grace,
In the hilarious twist of fate's embrace.

So gather round with cheer and glee,
For life's a jest, as you will see.
Our echoes of experience ring true,
In the ballad of me, and the ballad of you.

Colors of Contemplation

In a palette of thoughts, vibrant and bright,
We mix our mistakes, what a silly sight!
With hues of green for the envy we've felt,
And splashes of red from the laughter we've dealt.

Oh, the blues from our doubts in the night,
And the yellows where humor takes flight.
Every brushstroke tells a tale anew,
As we ponder our quirks, painted in view.

The canvas of life gets messy and wild,
With colors that brighten, just like a child.
For wisdom's a mess, but funny it seems,
As we color outside all the lines of our dreams.

So let's dip our brushes with glee and pride,
In this wild artwork, we'll take it in stride.
The colors of contemplation will cheer,
As we laugh at our journey, year after year.

Harmonies of Hope

In a tune where laughter finds its place,
We harmonize hope with a goofy face.
The melodies swirl, the rhythms collide,
With every note, our worries subside.

A misplayed chord, but who really cares?
Our serenade's rich with blunders and flares.
The chorus of life sings loud and clear,
As we dance through the chaos, shedding a tear.

With a harmony built on joy and jest,
Our voices unite, feeling truly blessed.
We improvise notes with a grin so wide,
As the harmonies of hope become our guide.

So join in the chorus, let's sing out loud,
In the symphony warm, we're all part of the crowd.
With laughter and hope, we'll never miss,
In this quirky concerto, pure bliss.

Bits of Brilliance

A spark of genius, or so we proclaim,
In the bits of brilliance, we play our game.
With moments of insight that make us laugh,
We stumble on wisdom like a comical path.

From brain farts that lead to the best of plans,
To quirky ideas that no one understands.
Every thought that slips from the tip of our tongue,
Has the potential to turn out quite fun.

So collect these nuggets, shiny and bright,
In the treasure chest of our crazy insight.
For brilliance is funny, and joyously so,
As we chuckle together at the things that we know.

Let's celebrate quirks, each peculiar quirk,
In this jiggle and wiggle, let's share a smirk.
For the bits of brilliance bring smiles each day,
In the hall of hilarity, come what may.

Threads of Insight

In a world of colorful ties,
I wear my thoughts like some disguise.
Each strand a chuckle, a tale or two,
Glimpses of wisdom, in laughs, imbue.

Tangled hair and silly puns,
Fashion statements, just for fun.
A twist of fate, a swipe of fate,
Dress my brain in love, don't be late!

Silly bands on arm they cling,
Every color dances, sings.
A wink of knowledge, that's the game,
Try wearing them, forget your name!

What if I trip on life's big stage?
I'll bounce right back, I'm not at wage.
With jumbled thoughts, I'll paint a scene,
A canvas bright, the quirkiest dream.

Adornments of Experience

On my wrist, a jolly glitch,
A mishmash memory, just a stitch.
Each bead a blunder, each charm a laugh,
Fashion advice from the Foolish Staff.

Want to know what not to do?
Just ask this crazy, colorful crew!
Beaded bands of blunders made,
Life is a circus, fun parade!

Worn out jokes and gestures sly,
Gems of folly, oh my, oh my!
Every twist holds laughter tight,
With every hug, I feel delight!

Experience wrapped, life's grappling hook,
In every mishap, take a look.
A giggle here, a snort over there,
Life's funny dance, we all must share.

Bands of Enlightenment

These bands on my wrist, what a sight!
Each one a joke, oh what delight!
They shimmer and shake with every cast,
A spark of wisdom, fun unsurpassed.

In a world right turned, I'll take the lead,
Mixing wisdom with silly creed.
Each loop and twist brings laughter near,
Lost in the fun, they disappear!

Facts and fables, jokes they tie,
Outsmart the frown, lift it high!
Like a riddle wrapped in glee,
Life's wisdom comes with a dose of spree.

Clad in blunders, I roam free,
Gentle nudge from memory spree.
These colorful bands, so quirky and spry,
Bring on the chuckles, let's all fly!

Wisdom Woven in Threads

Of all the laughter that we've shared,
Life's lightened up, so unprepared.
Threads of folly twist and weave,
A tapestry of joy, you wouldn't believe!

Riddles and rhymes, oh such plight,
Wisdom is stitched in every bite.
Each color tells of a funny tale,
Spinning yarns like we're on a sail.

Wrist-bound giggles, a silly affair,
Experience worn without a care.
This laughter band it holds my heart,
From life's great lessons, we can't depart.

In this fabric, we find our muse,
A playful glance, a joyful snooze.
Threads of laughter, swirls that blend,
Let's frolic together, on this we depend!

Echoes of Elder Wisdom

In the land of ancient lore,
Old folks share jokes by the door.
With canes like wands, they dance and spin,
Each punchline a lesson wrapped in a grin.

They say, 'Never trust a cat with your snack!'
Wisdom wrapped in laughter, a joyous knack.
'Kids these days, they text and they tap,
Lost in the void, oh, what a trap!'

With every chuckle, a truth unfolds,
Life's wisdom is funny, or so it holds.
'When life gives you lemons, make a pie!'
And laugh till the day we wave goodbye.

So cherish the giggles, the wisecracks too,
For echoes of wisdom come wrapped in boo-hoo.
With each little joke, we lighten our load,
A mind full of laughter is the ultimate road.

Sigils of the Seeker

A sage once wore a bright green hat,
Claimed it helped him chat with the cat.
With each weird sign, he'd preach and shout,
To seek is to find, without a doubt!

'Enhance your style with mismatched socks!
They hold the key, as hard as rocks.'
In every thread, a tale to tell,
Life's mysteries wrapped in mischief, oh so swell!

'Why bother with maps when you've got luck?'
The seeker grinned, a true-hearted pluck.
Adventure is found in the odd and bizarre,
Just follow the scent of the nearest candy bar!

So wear your quirks like badges of pride,
With giggles and guffaws, let joy be your guide.
In every quest, let laughter burst free,
For the seeker's treasure is pure comedy.

Tattoos of Thoughtfulness

On elbow and knee, they ink little jokes,
A reminder of laughs as life gently pokes.
'I've got a tattoo that's just a smile,'
It helps me stay thoughtful, even for a while.

'What's black and white and roams in the night?
A panda with issues, but that's all right!'
Each mark tells a story, a giggle or two,
On skin, warm wisdom wrapped in a hue.

Some ink birds that fly when you're feeling low,
Others dance like jelly where the wild thoughts go.
They tell tales of laughter, of wit and of glee,
A gallery of fun, don't you agree?

So wear your thoughts like a badge on your skin,
Each jot a reminder—the more, the grin!
Laughter's a canvas, the heart's quick to draw,
With thoughtful tattoos, we laugh without flaw.

Wraps of Realization

In the closet of truth, there lies a wrap,
Packed with wisdom and a warm zesty tap.
'No one's perfect, but that's no surprise!'
Wear it with humor, and you'll touch the skies.

With sleeves full of sun and pockets of cheer,
Embrace the quirks that keep you near.
For life's just a stage, a hilarious show,
When you trip on your shoes, let your laughter grow!

Every wrap tells a tale, both silly and warm,
Like dancing with socks when caught in a storm.
'The secret to life? Just ask a duck!'
With feathers and quacks, always tempting good luck!

So wrap yourself up in joy, pure delight,
For wisdom is found in a chuckle at night.
With each little wrap, come giggles and glee,
Embracing the fun, forever carefree!

Loop of Lessons

In the twist of rubber, thoughts align,
A circle of wisdom, oh so fine.
Each stretch a story, each snap a cheer,
Forget the old rules, let's make that clear.

With colors so bright, they dance on my wrist,
A reminder to laugh, can't let life be missed.
When I trip on my thoughts, and fall on my face,
These bands laugh with me, in the wild chase.

Around and around, lessons come and go,
Like a yo-yo in hand, they swing to and fro.
A comic delight, in the life we weave,
Witty reminders, if you dare to believe.

So join in the loop, let's swing and sway,
With a chuckle or two, we'll brighten the day.
In the rhythm of life, we'd rather be silly,
With every good laugh, it's a win, yes, really!

Handheld Heirlooms

Tiny treasures wrapped round and round,
Whispers of wisdom in colors abound.
These little heirlooms, they tickle the mind,
A giggle, a grin, the best finds are blind.

Each charm tells a tale, oh what a trip,
When life gets too serious, we take a good skip.
With laughter as magic, and mischief our friend,
We wear our own stories, on them we depend.

Hold tight to the giggles, let joy be your guide,
In the bustling moments, we wear it with pride.
An arsenal of fun, in a splendorous hue,
These handheld 'heirlooms' bring joy anew.

So gather your pals, let's frolic about,
With a quirk and a jest, there's never a doubt.
In this wild ride called life, let's liver it bright,
With laughter our armor, we'll rule through the night!

Armors of Awareness

Strapped tight on the wrist, with colors galore,
An armor of giggles, who could want more?
In moments of madness, when life starts to tilt,
These colorful bands remind us to guilt.

With a wink and a nudge, we ride through each blunder,
A signal to laugh, to hold back the thunder.
The quirkiest armor, our laughter the shield,
When seriousness hits, we joyfully wield.

It's more than a look; it's a badge of pure fun,
In the circus of life, together we run.
These moments of joy, they keep our hearts light,
In the battle of wisdom, it's humor that's right.

So let's raise our arms, in a funny salute,
To the lessons we learn, and the giggles we loot.
In this joyous adventure, what matters is glee,
And with laughter our armor, we'll always be free!

Tangles of Teachings

In a knot of colors, life's lessons weave,
A twist of pure laughter, it's hard to believe.
With each little tangle, a giggle or two,
In the mess of our thoughts, we find something true.

A clap of delight, when the shoelaces trip,
These comical tangles make hearts start to skip.
In the chaos we venture, we blur all the lines,
Finding joys in the chaos, our light now aligns.

So let's roll with the punches, when life gets insane,
With a sprinkle of chaos, we'll dance through the rain.
These tangles of teachings, they provide us a map,
To cherish each moment, and take life's big slap.

In this circus we spin, let laughter entwine,
Our lives as a tapestry, colorful design.
With every stitch woven, a tale to be spun,
In this tangle of joy, we're all having fun!

Heirlooms of Understanding

Old grandma says, wear this bright band,
It'll help you dance, keep you grand.
Wobbling around in a strange new pose,
Fell in the soup, now the whole town knows.

The dog wore one, thought it was a toy,
Chased his tail, what a silly boy!
Band on his paw, he claims he's a king,
But all we hear is him trying to sing.

Uncle Joe thought he'd give it a try,
Wrapped it too tight, oh my, oh my!
Turned his wrist green, now he's in chat,
"Was it the band? Or the stewed cat?"

So here's the lesson, if laughter won't cease,
These heirlooms of fun, bring joy, not peace.

Tokens of Truth

Wore a token, thought I looked wise,
A bird landed there, to my surprise.
Told me secrets, whispered so sweet,
"Your shoes are untied, now isn't that neat?"

That band on my wrist, it gleams in the sun,
I waved at a squirrel, made him run.
He stopped and he stared, then flipped me the bird,
Now I'm the proud owner of truth that's absurd.

A friend wore a band, thought it so cool,
Tried to impress, but he tripped on a stool.
The truth hit him hard, in a comical way,
"Now I'm wise too, since I'm flat on the bay!"

So let's wear these tokens, shiny and bright,
For truth can be funny, it's quite a delight!

Armlets of Awareness

With armlets on, I pose with pride,
But the truth is, I'm lost in the tide.
The map in my pocket, I zestfully threw,
Found a pizza slice, now what's a girl to do?

Awareness they say is a magical thing,
But I just got told I can't wear bling.
My armlet's so bright, it glints like the sun,
But my coffee's now cold, in the race that I run.

My buddy wears gold, claims he's a sage,
Got caught in the rain, now he's in a cage.
"Don't fret!" he yelled, with a squishy old grin,
"We all save the world with a splash of the gin!"

So listen, my friends, to these tales that flow,
The armlets of laughter bring warmth in the show.

Echoes in Fabric

In the swap meet, my fabric was bright,
Swapped it for wisdom, well, what a sight!
Echoes of laughter danced through the air,
Till I tripped over Bob, now how's that fair?

My patch with a saying, "Dance like a fool!"
Told me to giggle and break every rule.
But instead, I fell, and splashed in some pie,
Echoes of glee, as they heard my loud cry!

The fabric I wore caught the wind just right,
Twisted my head, like a tornado in flight.
"Just be yourself!" they said with a cheer,
But all I beheld was the inside of beer!

So here's to the echoes, bright in our life,
In pairs or on solo, avoid all the strife!

Insights Engraved

In the drawer lies a treasure,
Precepts we often measure.
With each band you wear with grace,
You'll navigate life's awkward pace.

Bright colors scream, decisions bold,
Like tasty truths, they're bought and sold.
With every twist, a lesson springs,
Like fish that dance on rubber rings.

Friendship, laughter, wisdom's jest,
Wear them tight, you'll feel the zest.
Even when life pulls a prank,
You'll find the truth behind the flank.

Witty quips and small delights,
Each one shines when day ignites.
These little bands, they love to tease,
On lazy days, they aim to please.

Bracelets of Belief

Chunky, sparkly, colors bright,
They whisper truths that spark delight.
Around your wrist, they dance and sway,
Adding charm to every day.

Don't let the skeptics pull you down,
With each bracelet, wear a crown.
A little jingle, a silly sway,
Bringing cheer in a quirky way.

For deep wisdom isn't stuffy,
It laughs and makes the world feel fluffy.
So twist and twirl in playful glee,
With each band, set your mind free.

Laugh at fortune when it teases,
Your wrist might hold the quirkiest breezes.
Grow wisdom that's a bit absurd,
Life's lessons wrapped in a vibrant word.

Classics of Clarity

Strapped to wrists like badges rare,
These charms unveil the truths we wear.
In fancy hues and woven dreams,
They guide you through life's quirky schemes.

Each knot and twist, a story spun,
With every laugh, life's never done.
A sprinkle of wisdom, wrapped so neat,
Life's overwhelming in a fun, sweet beat.

When the clouds roll in with burdens deep,
These classic threads, you know, won't weep.
Just give a jiggle and raise a toast,
Laughing at the worries you'll gladly host.

So put them on and take a chance,
Each bracelet calls for a silly dance.
Dance with clarity, feel the fun,
Life's wacky truths have just begun.

Bands of Being

Behold the bands that keep you sane,
With humor stitched in every grain.
They bounce and jiggle with every thought,
Embracing life's quirks, like it or not.

Colors clash like socks on a spree,
They mirror our souls, wild and free.
When life's a riddle that makes no sense,
These bands will offer comic suspense.

With every jolt and buzz of fun,
Life's crazy ride has just begun.
These magical loops won't lead you astray,
When all your plans go haywire today.

So wear them proudly, let them beam,
They'll fill your day with laughter and dream.
In every twist, wisdom's a thrill,
With each joyful band, embrace the chill.

www.ingramcontent.com/pod-product-compliance
Lightning Source LLC
Chambersburg PA
CBHW070003300426
43661CB00141B/168